Born with a BANG

Book One

The Universe Tells Our Cosmic Story

By Jennifer Morgan
Illustrated by Dana Lynne Andersen

Dawn Publications

Dedications

To the Universe in stones and stars and darkness and laughter. —JM

To the consummate original artist who has made all worlds beautiful: that Radiant Divine Intelligence whose center is everywhere, circumference nowhere. May our eyes be opened to behold the abounding magnificence of creation, the mysterious majesty of matter, energy and consciousness. —DLA

Copyright © 2002 Jennifer Morgan
Illustrations copyright © 2002 Dana Lynne Andersen

Illustration of the baby on page 6 by Anisa Claire Hovemann

Library of Congress Cataloging-in-Publication Data

Morgan, Jennifer, 1955-
 Born with a bang : the universe tells our cosmic story : book 1 / by
Jennifer Morgan.— 1st ed.
 p. cm. — (Sharing nature with children book)
 Includes bibliographical references.
 Summary: Presents a history of the universe, from the Big Bang to
the formation of Earth, in the form of a letter written by the
thirteen-billion-year-old universe itself to an Earthling.
 ISBN 1-58469-032-1 (pbk.) — ISBN 1-58469-033-X (hardback)
 1. Cosmology—Juvenile literature. [1. Cosmology. 2. Universe.]
I. Title. II. Series.
 QB983 .M67 2002
 523.1—dc21
                                    2001004623

Dawn Publications
12402 Bitney Springs Road
Nevada City, CA 95959
530-274-7775
nature@dawnpub.com
www.dawnpub.com

Manufactured by Regent Publishing Services,
Hong Kong Printed January 2016 in ShenZhen,
Guangdong, China

10 9
First Edition
Design and computer production by Andrea Miles

This glittering array of stars is a close look into the heart of our Milky Way by NASA's Hubble Heritage Team. The colors of stars reveal much about them. Most stars have an orange cast and are faint, as our Sun would be. The blue or greenish stars are young and hot, up to ten times hotter than our Sun, but are using up their fuel quickly and will live short lives. Small red stars are about half the temperature of our Sun, and live a long time. The "red giant" stars are ones that have almost used up their fuel, have swollen up, and are much cooler than previously. They are at the end of their lives.

About 13 billion years A.B.B.
(After Big Bang)

My Dearest Earthling,

You may not know me. We haven't talked before. I am the Universe and it's time for us to get to know each other. After all, I'm 13 billion years old now, give or take a few billion years.

And how old do you think you are? Nine? Thirteen? How about 13 billion years old too! You are a part of me—you are part of the Universe. You have never been separate from me. That's why I'm going to tell you a story about me, which is about you too.

There are many stories about how every-thing came to be. This story is based on discoveries by Earthling scientists. As they learn more, the story will change. I can't wait to share with you what I know so far.

Now, my dear Earthling, make yourself comfortable and let's begin at the very beginning . . .

Once you were a
tiny • speck

buried deep in the dark,

inside your mother.

But you couldn't stay small.

You grew and grew until
one day you were ready to
leave the darkness.
On that very special day,
your birthday, you were
born into the light.

I, too, had a special day when I was born.

But there was no light for me to be born into. I am the Universe. You were inside me from the very beginning—but not in your human form.

Like you, I started as a tiny speck. About 13 billion years ago, or so, I was smaller than a piece of dust under your bed. It's hard to imagine that I started out so small. But I did. And if you ask me where I came from, I would tell you that I don't know. It's the greatest of all mysteries. But there I was. Like you, I couldn't stay small.

I was bursting with wild and dazzling dreams of galaxies, stars and planets in radiant colors—

bright yellow,
molten red,
piercing blue.

In other dreams,
I saw strange creatures—

fish cruising deep blue seas,
insects alighting on flowers,
reptiles basking on hot rocks in the Sun,
birds swooping down on their prey,
and I saw you too, gazing at stars.

Could such amazing things really happen, I wondered?

Oh, how I wanted my dreams to happen. But how could they?
How could *you* happen?

Then I suddenly realized, I could BE the things in my dreams ☀

I could—

> *explode in a giant star,*
> *grow green in a thin blade of grass,*
> *roar as a lion and purr as a kitten,*
> *feel feelings like love, sadness, and wonder.*

Ah, yes, it began to dawn on me. Everything would have to come out of *me*. There was no other way. And everything would BE me.

But, I wondered, would I become—

> *worms with wings,*
> *foxes with fins,*
> *tulips with toes, or*
> *boulders with brains?*

I was puzzled. What forms would I like best? I didn't know. What if I tried and ended up making a big mess? Even though I was just a tiny speck, I wanted to try.

I decided to take the chance and do it. I summoned all my courage and took my first step.

I BURST into a grapefruit-sized fireball

of a Universe, packed with surging energy. It took only an instant. Space and time had just begun.

I was so bright, back then, I would have blinded you if you had eyes. But of course you didn't, yet.

I was so dense, I would have crushed your bones, if you had bones back then. But of course you didn't, yet.

I was so hot, I would have vaporized your muscles, if you had muscles back then. But of course you didn't, yet.

I would have to experiment and experiment before I could come up with eyes, bones and muscles that actually worked. But I'm getting way ahead of myself. Back then, you and everyone and everything else were still just energy packed inside me when I was a flaming little Universe. But you probably don't remember that. Or do you?

I couldn't hold myself at grapefruit size anymore. I was really ready to go for it.

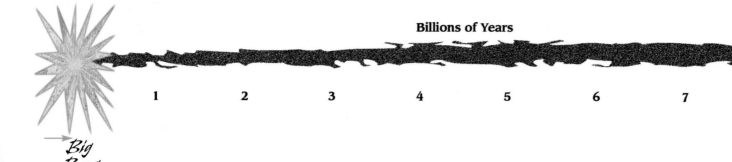

In a flash, space EXPLODED inside me with unimaginable power.

Like a gargantuan balloon, I blew up to the size of a galaxy. And it all happened faster than you can snap your fingers.

After I blew up, I kept growing, but more slowly. I had to find the right speed for a Universe. I could have died if everything had not been just right. If I had grown just a bit more slowly, my own gravity would have overpowered me and squashed me into nothingness. If I had grown just a bit faster, I would have blown apart and disappeared into nothingness. That would have been the end of our story. No galaxies, no turtles, and no you. But everything WAS just right.

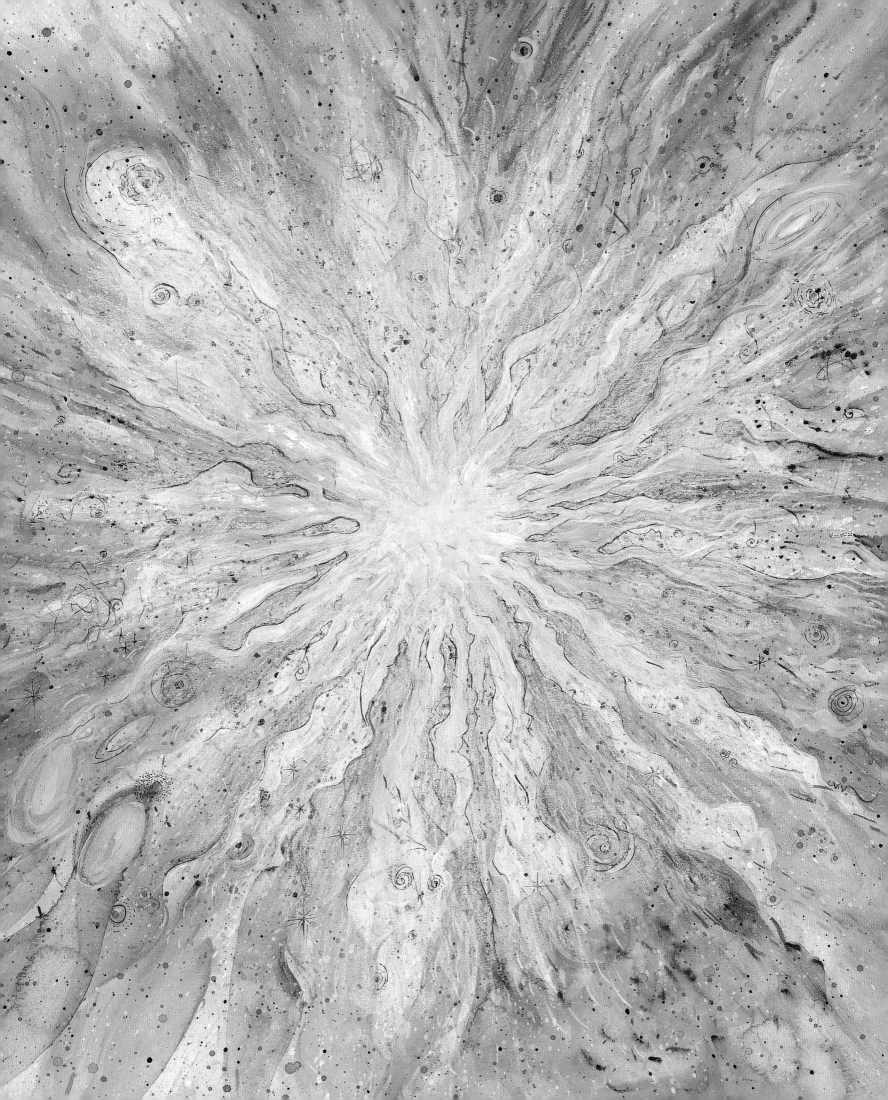

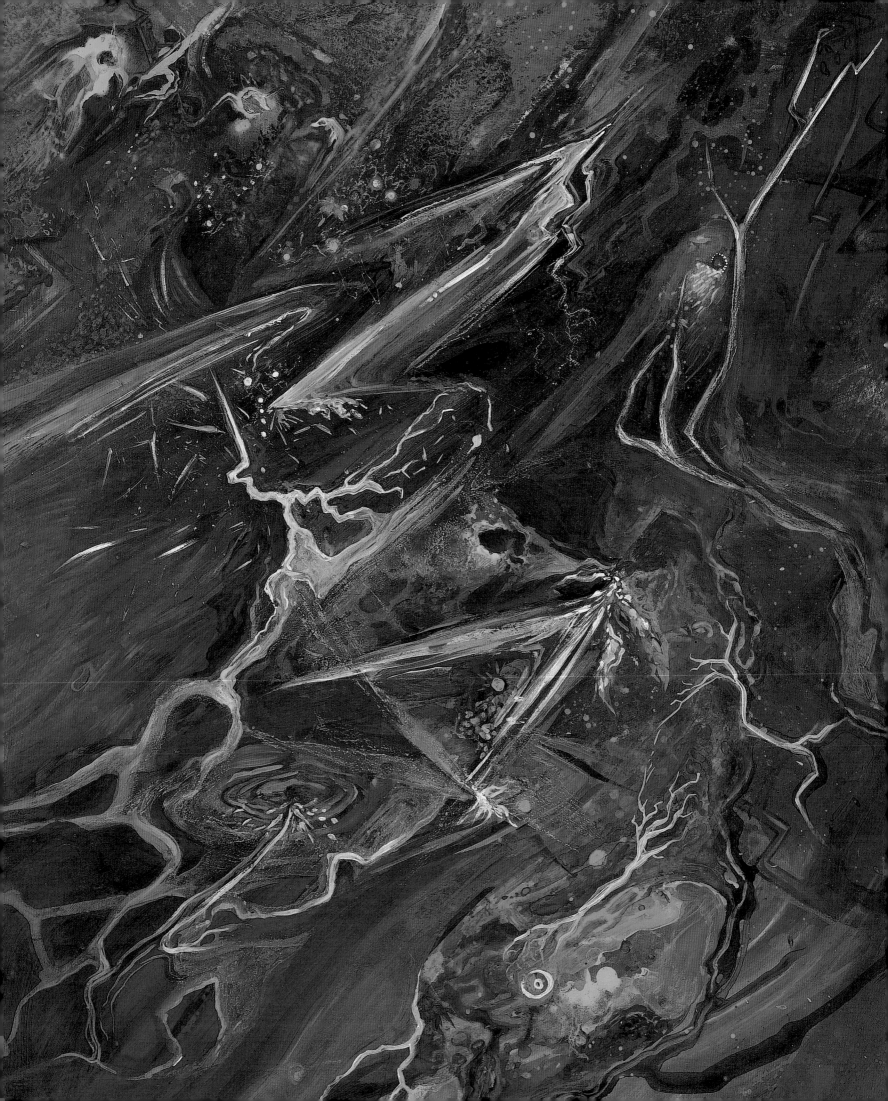

Big Bang

I was hardly a tidy young Universe. If I had a human mother, she would have scolded me for all my clutter and confusion. And I'm not just talking about dirty socks on the cosmic floor. It was utter bedlam! When I was a fraction of a second old, I was already a mess.

Hotter than one trillion degrees, I was blazing with the heat of billions of suns. Suddenly, gigantic glowing bolts of energy flashed everywhere and shrank into teensy *things*. Oh no! What had I done? Actually, I had done something incredible.

Yes!

I had turned energy into the very first THINGS—tiny *particles*.

Particles are the invisible bits of stuff that everything is made of. Maybe my dreams could come true. Maybe I could turn myself into stars and grass and lions and kittens and tulips and boulders. Maybe I could be you, too.

Science Concept: Energy into matter (see page 41)

But—oh blast! A frustrating thing kept happening.

Every time I turned energy into a particle, its exact opposite, an anti-particle, would appear.

These pairs weren't friendly. In fact, they were enemies that destroyed each other every time they met. I had barely begun my adventure and already I was out of control. Two sides were at war, yet both were part of me.

In the beginning, they were equally matched and kept zapping each other. So I made more—billions more. And then, amazingly, for every billion particles that were zapped by anti-particles, I was able to make one extra particle. The particles were winning! So I made more and more and more.

Then I stopped. I had enough basic bits of stuff to build myself into the Universe you know today. And guess what! The number of these particles has stayed the same ever since. Everything, including your body, is made out of those same particles that I made long, long ago.

But I'm getting ahead of myself again. Back then, when I had just finished making particles, I looked like a huge glowing fog. Zapped particles and anti-particles hadn't disappeared; they had turned into light. That's when I knew that even though things might seem to die, they never really end. They just change form. After all, everything is part of me and always will be. I am particles *and* I am light.

It's hard to believe, but I was still less than one second old! So much was happening at breakneck speed.

Science Concept: Matter survives the first massive extinction (see page 41)

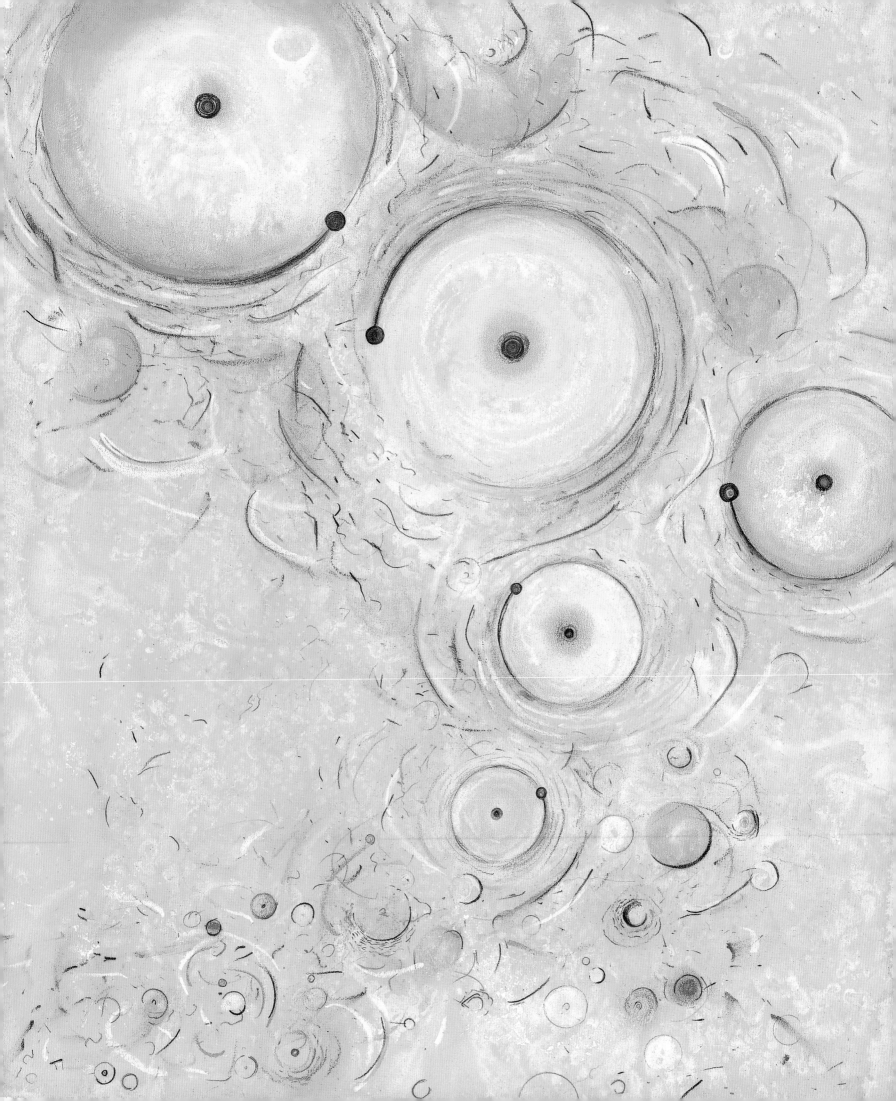

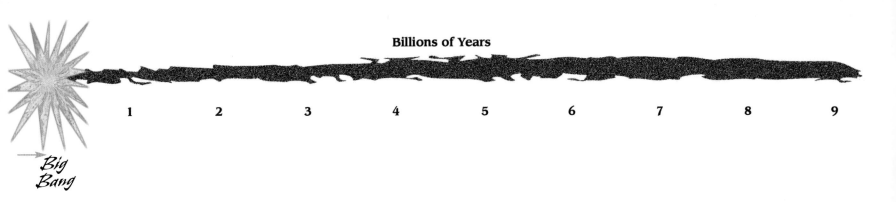

Young particles raced around and around inside me, dizzily tumbling and crashing into one another like kids playing on a couch. By the time I was about 300,000 years old, I was pretty cool—only about 3,000 degrees.

Suddenly another amazing thing happened—it might have been accidental, but I don't think so. I was just the right temperature for bunches of particles to join together, and when they joined together they morphed into *very different things!* They were small but very important. They were kind of like Lego pieces—building blocks that I could use later for making bigger things.

I had made my very first *atoms*. They were atoms of hydrogen.

Was I proud of creating hydrogen atoms? You bet I was. I was just a kid Universe, and already I had hit my first home run. You would have cheered me on if you had a voice back then. But of course you didn't, yet.

Hydrogen atoms are still really important to me. Every gulp of water that slides down your throat is made of hydrogen that was created by me billions of years ago. Of course, back then there was no water, yet.

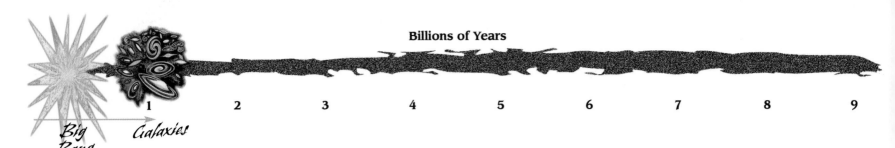

Billions of Years

Big Bang Galaxies

The hydrogen fog began to ripple and clump together into wavy strings. Gravity pulled these strings together into globs. As the globs got bigger, the gravity got stronger, which made the globs get even bigger. The bigger they got, the hotter they got. Then—wow!—one of my dreams began to come true.

These enormous hydrogen globs started igniting into Mother Stars!

One here, one there—soon there were huge Mother Stars everywhere. Gigantic groups of Mother Stars spiraled in space.

I was shaping myself into *galaxies*.

Science Concepts: Star formation (see page 41) and galaxies (see page 42)

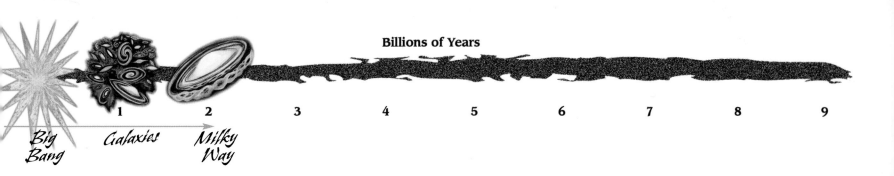

There were billions of galaxies, each with billions of stars, spinning and sparkling like jewels in the black night.

In the center of your Milky Way, my gravity became so powerful that it turned into a *black hole*. Oh, oh! Everything near the black hole—stars, dust clouds and even light—got trapped and sucked in. It all swirled down into the black hole's mysterious dark depths, just as water swirls and disappears down a bathtub drain.

Mysterious black holes appeared at the center of many galaxies ●〜

Where did all that stuff go? Is it stuck inside? Did I do something wrong? Or are black holes really secret passageways into other Universes? All that stuff has to be somewhere because nothing ever really disappears.

After a while, the black holes sucked up all the nearby stars that their gravity could reach. Then they settled down and became quiet. Your Milky Way, and billions of other galaxies too, were growing up.

Mind you, my dear Earthling, your Milky Way is one tiny neighborhood in my vast expanse. Even though your galaxy is very special, I care equally for all my galaxies! Every one of them is part of me. In fact, they all ARE me.

Science Concept: Black holes (see page 42)

27

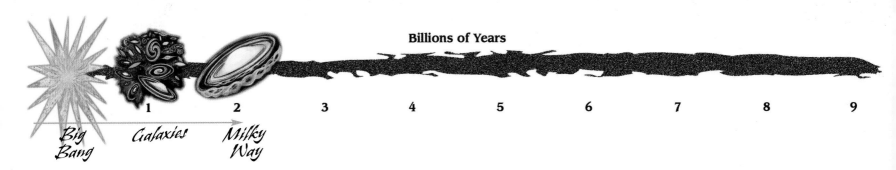

Luckily, lots and lots of young stars hadn't been sucked into black holes. In one of the Milky Way's spiraling arms, one Mother Star very important to you grew into a shimmering majestic giant. She lived long before your Sun was born and was much, much bigger than your Sun would be. Inside her enormous blazing belly, she did something incredible!

Your Mother Star mixed together bunches of hydrogen and baked them at three billion degrees into lots of different new elements, or building blocks.

One of these new elements was *carbon*. One day, chains of carbon called DNA would carry instructions from one generation to the next for how each living thing should grow.

Another new element was *oxygen*. One day, oxygen would combine with hydrogen to make one of my most magnificent things, water. And where would you be without oxygen to breathe and water to drink?

Yet another was *calcium*. Calcium can be really hard stuff. How useful for making bones!

Carbon, oxygen and calcium can't be made on Earth, because it's much too cool. Every atom of these elements was fused inside a colossal Mother Star. Was I proud of her new elements? You bet I was!

Science Concept: Elements (see page 42)

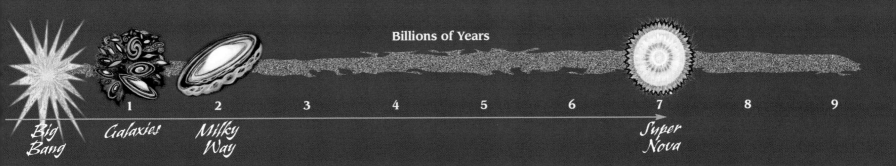

Before your own star could be born—the one you call the Sun—your Mother Star had to die.

Your Mother Star ripped herself apart in a massive explosion—a *supernova*.

Tiny specks of carbon, oxygen and calcium, and all the other new building blocks she made, blasted into space and cooled into stardust. Her stardust was the same stardust that would one day come together to create you. You are made of stardust – every bit of it exploded from your ancient Mother Star who no longer lives. I was about 7 billion years old when she died.

Inside the cloud of stardust, a little gravity tugged from each speck, making them gently stick together in little clumps. The little clumps clumped together into bigger clumps. The bigger clumps crashed into each other and stayed together. They swirled into a disk shape, faster and faster, hotter and denser, tighter and brighter, until finally—

Science Concept: Supernovas (see page 42)

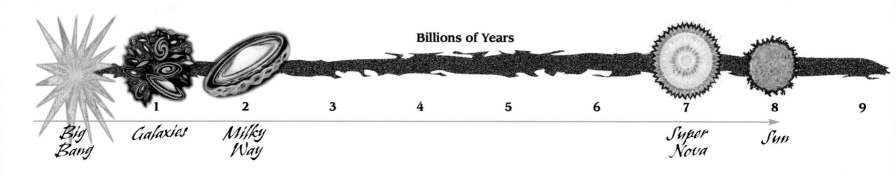

Whoosh!

Your Sun flared into life! Born, too, from clumps of stardust were nine young planetary pups!

The planets tagged along after father Sun. But they were smaller and had no light of their own. Planets depend on the Sun's generosity, just as human children depend on their parents for food and shelter. Oh, how I delighted as your Sun sent light and warmth to its planets.

By now you know, everything within me is giving and receiving. And when things team up with each other, they morph into even more spectacular forms, just as—

> *Particles create hydrogen by sticking together,*
> *Hydrogen clouds compress themselves into stars,*
> *And stars gather in gleaming galaxies.*

To use human language, you might say that I, the Universe, am loving myself through everything that is playing and working together, even the tiny particles teaming up to form you. There I go again, talking about Earthlings long before they existed. Do you want to know what has always propelled my adventure forward? It's giving and receiving. And it's playing and working together.

   Science Concept: Solar systems (see page 42)

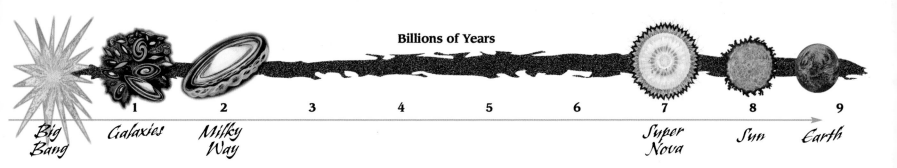

The third pup inside the young planetary pack, your Earth, was a burning red ball of molten stardust.

I was about eight and a half billion years old when your Earth was born. She was a high energy young pup, cruising around your Sun. Erupting volcanoes spewed steam and other gases. The steam turned to rain, and the rain formed vast oceans. Other gases rose up and became the air. Lightning storms zapped her seas. Meteors and comets crashed into her for millions of years.

Slowly, slowly, she cooled down and formed a firm crusty surface. A hungry young planet, she drank light and warmth from her golden Sun, her source of life in the midst of cold, dark space. Sun and Earth began their rhythmic dances of day and night; spring, summer, fall, and winter.

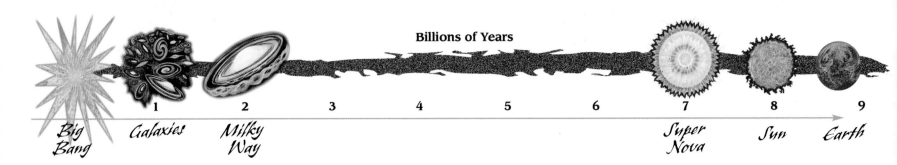

The ocean bubbled and boiled. Hot red rocks oozed up through rips in the ocean floor.

What would I, the Universe, turn myself into next? This was exciting! I remembered my wild and dazzling dreams of galaxies and stars and planets. Now I had them, or maybe I should say, now I *was* them.

But wait. I remembered another dream too. I remembered creatures slicing through water, creeping on plants, crawling on rocks, soaring on winds, and gazing at stars. You were there, too. Oh, how I longed to become creatures, including you. Would this be a good place for creatures to begin to twitch and multiply?

Did I have enough building blocks to turn myself into creatures?

Ah, let's see. I had made hydrogen a long, long time ago. And inside Mother Stars I had made carbon, oxygen, calcium, and a whole bunch of other building blocks. And then I had brought hydrogen and oxygen together to form water. Maybe I was ready.

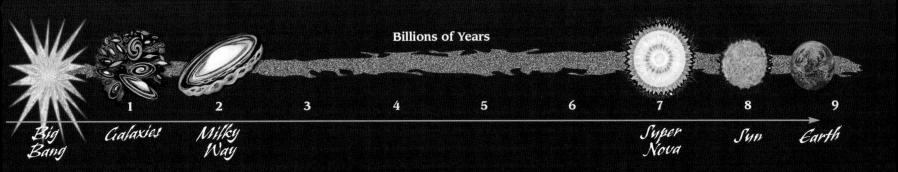

Of course, dear Earthling,
my story—OUR story—doesn't end here.

So much still had to happen before I could turn myself into you.

In my next story, your planet Earth comes alive. But that will have to wait for another day. Until we talk again, I send you my very best from the cosmos. Remember, I am always with you. My sweet Earthling, I will tell you a secret: I'm even closer to you than that. It's true—I am you.

Love,

The Universe

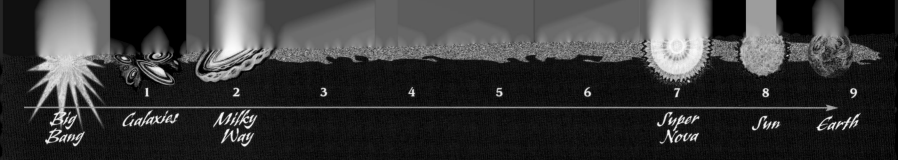

P.S. Now that you've heard my story, you can see how much I learned over my first eight and a half billion years. Maybe you have learned some of the same things too!

I learned . . .

- to turn a dream into reality.

- that even giant things start out small.

- that to build things I need building blocks.

- that I love to experiment.

- that there are special times for doing things, or I would lose my chance.

- that I couldn't be creative without being destructive too.

- to be patient.

- that I love variety.

- that my life is uncertain—and therefore a great adventure.

- that when parts of me "die," they don't really come to an end, they just change form.

- that I really love to morph into different forms.

- that I am a "uni-verse," which means "one song."

How did I learn all these things about myself? Earthling scientists, and a lot of other Earthlings like poets, artists, and spiritual leaders, have been a big help. Of course, don't forget that all Earthlings are really me looking back on myself so I can discover more about who I am. Even you. Talk to you soon!

Discoveries by Earthling Scientists

The Big Bang *(page 16)* Scientists estimate that between 12 and 15 billion years ago, the Universe flared into being in a massive explosion known as the "Big Bang." Time, space and matter all began in the Big Bang. Scientists think this is so because galaxies are moving farther apart. Another way of saying this is that the space between galaxies is growing larger. Our Universe has been expanding from the very beginning. Looking backward in time, the galaxies we observe today would move closer and closer to each other, to a time when they were compressed into a volume far smaller than a grain of sand. Though this may have been true about the Universe we can observe, we don't know the size or shape of the entire Universe. There may be other Universes, but we only know about our own.

Energy into matter *(page 19)* The first particles, or matter—the material stuff out of which our Universe is made—was converted out of energy. Albert Einstein, the famous scientist, showed that matter can become energy, and energy can become matter.

Matter survives the first massive extinction *(page 20)* Within the first second after the Big Bang, particles and anti-particles were formed out of energy, annihilating each other instantly upon contact. Particles gained a slight advantage. For every one billion pairs of particles and anti-particles, there was one extra particle. The extra particle survived. Scientists do not know why there was one extra particle. Without those surviving particles, the material Universe would have ended before it was one second old. The entire material Universe was created from these surviving particles. The amount of material in the Universe was set for all time.

Formation of hydrogen atoms *(page 23)* The infant Universe was very hot—well over 10,000 trillion trillion degrees (see the timeline below). Particles called "quarks" rampaged wildly in a dense particle soup, unable to come together to form anything. When it was still a tiny fraction of a second old, the Universe cooled down to 10 trillion degrees. At that temperature, quarks came together to form protons and neutrons. By the time the Universe was three minutes old, it had cooled to 10 billion degrees. At that temperature, protons and neutrons came together to form helium nuclei and all the protons left over were hydrogen nuclei. After about 300,000 years, when the Universe cooled to about 3,000 degrees, protons and another kind of particle, electrons, joined together to form the first atoms— hydrogen and helium. Hydrogen is the simplest atom with one proton and one electron. Helium has two protons, two neutrons, and two electrons. This photo (top right) from the BOOMERANG Project's balloon-borne telescope over Antarctica shows the Universe at that young age—when protons and electrons came together to form the first atoms. The Universe was already beginning to form into globs that might later form into stars. It is possible to photograph events that happened

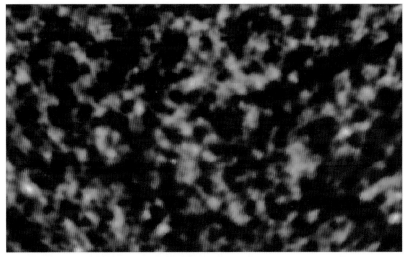

long ago if they are extremely far away, because it takes that long for the light to reach Earth.

Star formation *(page 24)* These two photos taken by NASA's Hubble Space Telescope show stars in different stages of being born. On the left, stars are forming from huge pink "molecular clouds" of hydrogen. Gravity is causing clumps to condense, ignite and glow inside the bright gaseous "pillars" within the clouds. Above and to the left of the clouds is a cluster of young stars. They have generated a "stellar wind" of

radiation that "blows" the gas clouds away. Above the cluster is a blue super-giant star surrounded by a ring of heavier atoms. In the photo on the right, a gas cloud glows as stars form.

Galaxies *(page 24)* This photo from NASA's Hubble Space Telescope shows two spiral galaxies in near-collision. Scientists predict that the smaller one on the right does not have the energy to escape the gravitational pull of the larger one on the left, and that eventually they will merge. It is thought that many galaxies, including our Milky Way, were assembled by smaller galaxies merging together over billions of years.

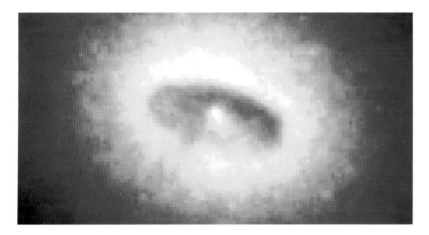

Black holes (page 27) Black holes are probably the strangest objects in the Universe. Their gravity is so strong that dust, stars, and even light can never escape. Scientists don't know what happens to things that get sucked in. Perhaps they are crushed into an infinitely small place, or perhaps they travel through a "worm hole" into another Universe. Some black holes are formed when stars die. Others form in the centers of galaxies. Black holes may appear either black, because light cannot escape, or bright, because the stuff that is falling in heats up and glows. This photo from NASA's Hubble Space Telescope shows a galaxy composed of hundreds of billions of stars with a black hole in the center. The hole is illuminated by matter that is heating up under intense gravity as it falls into the hole. The darker ring around the center feeds matter into the hole.

Elements *(page 28)* Three elements—hydrogen, helium and a small amount of lithium—were created in the Big Bang or shortly thereafter. Hydrogen makes up about 90 percent of the number of atoms in the Universe and helium makes up about 8 percent. The other 89 elements, many critical to life, were created inside of stars. They make up less than one percent of

the number of atoms in the Universe. It is literally true that humans are made from stardust.

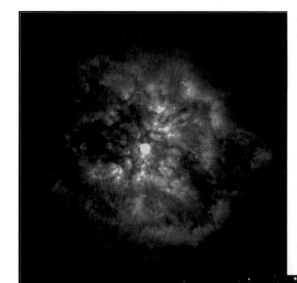

Supernova *(page 31)* All stars die. Some die calmly. Some die violently in explosions called supernovas. To die in a supernova, a star must be at least eight times the mass of our Sun. Once the star uses up its hydrogen fuel, it begins to expand into a red giant. The core gets hotter and hotter, fusing hydrogen and helium together into more complicated elements such as oxygen, carbon, and calcium, and 86 other elements. Then the center collapses and the star explodes in a supernova. Its newly-created elements are scattered in space, to be recycled into new stars. In this way, stars are not too different from other cycles of nature, such as when plants and animals die and send their elements back to the soil from which other plants and animals grow. The photo at left from NASA's Hubble Space Telescope is probably about to go supernova. It is a great fireball ejecting clumps into space at over 100,000 miles per hour. At right is the famous Crab Nebula, the remains of a spectacular supernova that was recorded by Chinese astronomers in the year 1054. This photo was taken at the European Southern Observatory's very large telescope in Chile.

Solar system *(page 32)* This NASA photo (right) shows our turbulent Sun. The Sun's energy is generated in the core where it is 15 million degrees. Our Sun and its planets were formed from a single large disk of dust. The four inner rocky planets—Mercury, Venus, Earth, and Mars—were molten at first, then developed rocky surfaces with metallic cores. The four outer gas giants—

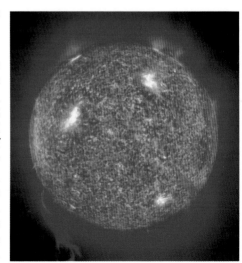

Jupiter, Saturn, Uranus, and Neptune—formed in the cooler outer regions. Little Pluto may have been formed out of material not used in the gas giants, or it was captured later. Scientists think they can see solar systems being born, such as in this photo from NASA. It shows a disk of gas and dust about the size of our solar system that appears to be condensing into a new solar system. However, other powerful stars in its neighborhood may cause much of the cloud to evaporate before planets can condense.

Earth before life (page 35) Before life began, Earth was a dangerous and turbulent place, but the commotion was actually organizing the elements for life. Meteors crashing to Earth brought more building blocks for life. Volcanoes on land and under the sea brought up more elements in the molten lava. This activity helped form the Earth's iron core and brought lighter elements to the surface. Even the endless lightning storms that electrified the oceans may have been crucial for life. Earth's temperature was just right for water to exist in its liquid, gaseous and frozen forms. Over time, the elements would organize even further, into the very first forms of life.

A Timeline of Triumphs in the Universe's Life

Time equals zero (13 billion years ago). The Universe is born when space and time are born inside of the tiny speck. Everything in the Universe we observe today was compressed inside that speck. We don't know what existed before that.

Bang! (less than 1 second old). The laws of physics as we know them began when the Universe had expanded to the size of a grapefruit, and is 10^{-36} seconds old. (This is the scientific way to write a tiny number that has a 1 that is 36 places to the *right* of the decimal, or .0000000000000000000000000000000001. Notice that there are 35 zeroes, or 36 minus one. This is the same as saying one trillion trillion trillionth of a second). Temperature begins at near infinity degrees and drops to 10^{28} degrees. (This is the scientific way of writing a huge number that has a one with 28 zeroes to the *left* of the decimal, or 10,000 trillion trillion degrees.) The Universe is about 10^{72} times denser than water. Then, in a tiny fraction of a second, the Universe increases in size about 10^{50} times, up to the size of a galaxy. This is what is commonly known as *inflation*, or the "Big Bang." At the end of inflation, particles and anti-particles flash into being. A slight imbalance of particles and anti-particles develops. For every one billion pairs of particles and anti-particles that destroy each other, one extra particle survives.

From 1 second to 3 minutes old. The Universe cools down to 10 billion degrees. Protons and neutrons come together to form helium nuclei. All protons left over form hydrogen nuclei.

300,000 years old. The Universe cools to 3,000 degrees, cool enough for electrons to settle down and join with hydrogen and helium nuclei to form the first atoms. The Universe clears and space turns transparent.

One billion years old. Galaxies, or large groups of stars, begin to take shape and have been forming ever since. Early primal stars, or Mother Stars, form out of hydrogen clouds. They fuse hydrogen into many other elements including carbon, oxygen, and calcium. When they explode as supernovas, their stardust forms into new stars and planets. The new stars and planets contain more complicated elements that open the way for the evolution of life. Many generations of stars have been born and have died. That process continues today.

Two billion years old. The Milky Way forms. The oldest star clusters in the Milky Way date back to when the universe was probably one billion years old. They joined with new clusters and the Milky Way grew over a long time into the galaxy it is today.

Seven billion years old. Our Mother Star may have gone supernova around this time, although scientists cannot pinpoint a time. There may have been more than one Mother Star whose dust formed our solar system. We don't know.

Eight billion years old. The solar system forms, starting as a cloud of gas and dust. The cloud collapses into a shrinking disk. Gravity pulls clumps of matter together and the Sun is born in the center of the disk when nuclear fusion starts up. Nuclear fusion, the fusion of hydrogen into helium, makes stars shine.

Eight and a half billion years old. About 500 million years after the Sun began nuclear fusion, the planets formed in the outer parts of the disk. The third planet, Earth, orbits the Sun in a position that's just right for life: not too hot and not too cold.

Glossary

Anti-particle A particle having exactly the opposite properties of a particle. For example, the anti-particle to an electron, which has a negative charge, is a positron, which is identical to an electron but has a positive charge. When a positron and an electron meet, they annihilate each other. Few anti-particles exist today compared to the beginning of the Universe, when an almost equal number of particles and anti-particles existed.

Atom The smallest "piece" of an element. It consists of a core, or "nucleus," made up of protons and neutrons, surrounded by a cloud of orbiting electrons.

Black hole An object with gravity so powerful that nothing, not even light, can escape. Black holes are at the center of most galaxies. Collapsing stars can also produce black holes.

Calcium A soft, silver-white element created at very high temperatures inside stars and found on Earth in limestone, marble, chalk, milk, vegetables, and animal bones. It becomes hard in bones when it combines with other elements.

Carbon An element found in rocks, diamonds, graphite pencils, and all living things. Although it makes up less than a millionth of the mass of planet Earth, carbon is the building block of life because it can form long chains that store genetic information.

Electrons Negatively charged particles in atoms that circulate around the nucleus, or center of the atom.

Element Any of the basic substances of nature which cannot be broken down chemically.

Galaxy A group of billions of stars, gas, and dust bound together by their gravitational pull. The Milky Way, a medium-size galaxy, has about 400 billion stars.

Helium Along with hydrogen nuclei, helium nuclei were formed before the Universe was three minutes old. After 300,000 years, electrons joined the nuclei to form helium atoms. Helium atoms have two protons, two neutrons and two electrons. Helium makes up nearly eight percent of the total number of atoms in the Universe.

Hydrogen The first element created within the newly born Universe, hydrogen is the lightest element from which all other elements were formed. A flammable, colorless, odorless gas, hydrogen makes up 90 percent of the number of atoms of the Universe. The simplest atom, it has one proton and one electron.

Mass Amount of matter forming a body. On Earth, the mass of a body is equal to its weight.

Matter The substance that occupies space and from which all things are made. Matter is a form of energy, as explained by Albert Einstein's famous equation $E=MC^2$, that is, energy equals mass times the speed of light multiplied by itself. A very little bit of mass equals a very large amount of energy. If the mass in a baseball were converted into energy, it would power a city of one million people for one month.

Neutron A particle found in the core, or nuclei, of atoms that has no electrical charge.

Nucleus The central part of an atom, which is formed by protons and neutrons. Protons have a positive charge, and neutrons have no charge, giving nuclei a positive charge. "Nuclei" is the plural of nucleus.

Oxygen An element that is a colorless, odorless, tasteless gas. Oxygen makes up one fifth of the Earth's atmosphere and is essential to most forms of life.

Particle A tiny, individual component of matter. Different particles behave differently according to their mass, spin, and electrical charge. Quarks, leptons, protons, neutrons and electrons are examples of particles.

Proton Found in the core, or nucleus, of an atom, a proton has a positive electrical charge. The nucleus of a hydrogen atom is made up of one proton.

Supernova The explosion of a massive star at the end of its life. When a star dies in a supernova, the explosion creates and blasts newly formed elements into space. Eighty-nine elements—such as carbon, oxygen, calcium, iron and gold—can only be created inside of stars. The elements made in stars make up just one percent of the total number of atoms in the Universe, but are critical to life.

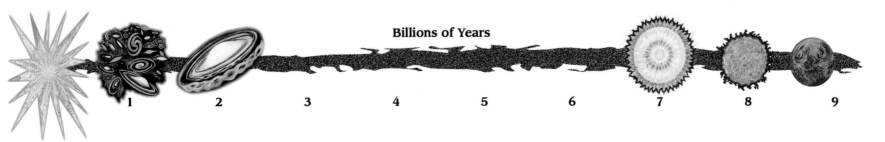

Letters from two formations of stardust — Thomas Berry and Brian Swimme

Thomas Berry, Ph.D., is a cultural historian. He is author of The Great Work *and* The Dream of the Earth, *seminal works that have had a profound influence on the field of cosmology. Brian Swimme, Ph.D., is a mathematical cosmologist researching the nature of evolutionary dynamics. He is author of* The Universe Story. *(See www.brianswimme.org.)*

Through human beings, the Universe has begun to remember and tell its own story of being born and growing up. That the Universe can now tell its story through Ms. Morgan's voice and Ms. Andersen's art, is the culmination of centuries of scientific inquiry.

In *Born With a Bang*, we can experience the Universe in its full grandeur, and deeply sense the numinous presence that pervades the entire world about us. To awaken to the wonder of the Universe is to appreciate life in its full excitement. We might also develop a new capacity to relate to each other. A reverence for the Universe is the beginning of true reverence for the divine and for each other.

Nowhere is the telling of this story more important than to children. Human life will be very different if our children learn the story. The first obligation of one generation to the next is to bring together Universe and child so that the Universe is fulfilled in the child and the child is fulfilled in the Universe.

We need to hear the story from our cradle days through all stages of our lives, for we refer to the Universe for our origin and ultimate destiny. It's time to reshape our thinking inside of this context. Indeed, our future depends on it.

—Thomas Berry

Born With a Bang is a healthy retreat from the world of unthinking consumerism to a world of cosmological identification. The great power of this story is its personification of the Universe and all the beings within it. We in the modern industrial world find this difficult to absorb. We have been educated to think of the Universe as an "it," to think of a tree as an "it," and to regard everything non-human as something that exists for our use rather than for its own intrinsic purpose. This "I-it" orientation dominates our schools, our businesses, our manufacturing processes, and our politics.

But in the magic of Jennifer's story and Dana's art, we begin to feel something very different. We imagine, even if only for a short moment, that we live in a personal Universe, a Universe that cares. A Universe that is filled with passion. A Universe that delights in its work, even the work of giving birth to us. Suddenly, even if only for the briefest instant, we have the feeling that we BELONG. And that one flash of an insight can provide a person with an entirely different orientation in the Universe.

Inside this story, we dare to imagine. What if we are not here just to get a good job? What if our existence is more significant than the things we buy? What if we truly belong here because the Universe has labored for 13 billion years to bring us into being? What if the ultimate meaning of our brief lives is the way in which we enable the care that gave birth to us to extend out through human hands in the great work of building a vibrant, compassionate Earth community?

—Brian Swimme

Resources

Books for Children and Teachers

Big Bang: The Story of the Universe by Heather Couper and Nigel Henbest, illustrated by Luciano Corbella. Clear and well illustrated, using scientific terms, this book is for adults and children over ten.

Earth Story by Eric Maddern, illustrated by Leo Duff. A magically-told story about Earth's formation.

Happy Birthday Universe! A Cosmic Curriculum for Children by Kym Farmer, Sycamore Hollow Retreat Center, Celina, TN 38551, 931-243-4170. Kym@sycamorehollow.com. An excellent curriculum for K through 6th grade.

Life Story: The Story of Life on Our Earth from its Beginning up to Now by Virginia Lee Burton. Explains evolution as a play.

My Place in Space by Robin and Sally Hirst. A bus driver asks little Henry where he lives and gets more of an answer than he expected.

Space Encyclopedia. Couper, Heather and Nigel Henbest. A comprehensive, well-illustrated encyclopedia.

The Kingfisher Young People's Book of Space by Martin Redfern. This beautifully illustrated book explains space, the solar system, and cosmic questions.

The Universe at Your Fingertips by Andrew Fraknoi. Ninety ready-to-use teaching activities for any age group.

Books for adults

A Vedantin's View of Christian Concepts by Swami Dayananda Saraswati and Prof. Helmut Girndt. A fascinating conversation compares how eastern and western views of God shape our understanding of the Universe.

A Walk Through Time by Sidney Liebes, Elisabet Sahtouris, and Brian Swimme. Mostly tells the story of Earth, but with a prologue by Swimme that covers the time before Earth.

Lonely Hearts of the Cosmos: The Story of the Scientific Quest for the Secrets of the Universe by Dennis Overbye. The adventures of astrophysicists that led to the discovery of quasars, black holes, and dark matter.

The Dream of the Earth by Thomas Berry. A seminal book by an eminent cultural historian about what it means to be part of an alive Universe.

The Elegant Universe: Superstrings, Hidden Dimensions, and the Quest for the Ultimate Theory by Brian Greene. Greene explains how superstring theory may reconcile general relativity and quantum mechanics.

The Essential Aurobindo by Robert McDermott. The writings of a great Indian thinker on the meaning of evolution.

The First Three Minutes: A Modern View of the Origin of the Universe by Steven Weinberg. A classic by a Nobel prize-winning physicist.

The Great Work by Thomas Berry. How cosmology calls us to experience the wonder of the Universe and move away from a commodity view of the natural world.

The Sacred Depths of Nature by Ursula Goodenough. Sheds luminous clarity on the quest for meaning within modern science.

The Universe is a Green Dragon by Brian Swimme. An eloquent, mind-bending discussion about the dynamics of the Universe.

The Universe Story: From the Primordial Flaring Forth to the Ecozoic Era, A Celebration of the Unfolding of the Cosmos by Brian Swimme and Thomas Berry. The best narrative of the Universe story, blending science with spirituality.

The Whole Shebang by Timothy Ferris. An overview of cosmological theory by a highly respected popular science writer.

Videos

Amazing Earth with Brian Swimme

Blue Planet by the Smithsonian Institute and NASA

Canticle to the Cosmos with Brian Swimme

Creation of the Universe with Timothy Ferris

Hidden Heart of the Cosmos with Brian Swimme

Universe Story with Thomas Berry

Other Resources

Astronomical Society of the Pacific, San Francisco, CA., www.aspsky.org, (800)335-2624. Books, posters, slides, and maps.

Astronomy Magazine, 800-533-6644. A great resource for amateur astronomers, including developments in cosmology.

Astronomy.com. Daily news, photo galleries, star charts, shopping, telescope information.

CosmicVoyage.com. An online museum of cosmology, modern and ancient.

NASA.gov. Beautiful Hubble space pictures, explanations, and activities for children.

Scientific American Magazine, 800-333-1199. One of the best cosmology information sources.

Space-Talk.com. Message board for astronomy, space and related topics; all posts get archived.

Jennifer Morgan's work as a storyteller, author, educator and environmental advocate flows out of her love of the natural world and cosmology. As former director of the Northeast Organic Farming Association of New Jersey, she started numerous educational and marketing programs for farmers and consumers, both locally and nationally. Currently she is an adjunct staff member at Genesis Farm, teaching the Sacred Universe Story. A portion of Ms. Morgan's royalties from the sale of this book are donated to earth literacy centers. Her storytelling evolved from bedtime stories for her son who wanted to know more and more, even the texture of the edge of the Universe. She believes that our cosmology stories fundamentally shape us—our relationships, our work, our play, our culture, our institutions, our everything.

Dana Lynne Andersen, M.A., is a multi-media artist, playwright and teacher with degrees in philosophy and consciousness studies. Her paintings, often very large in size, explore the swirling forces of energy that underlie matter and seek to reveal life's numinous mystery. She believes that as our "depth perception" expands—billions of galaxies discovered in our lifetime!—it is also essential to expand perception inwardly to the vastness within. She is founder of Awakening Arts, a network of artists who "affirm the noble purpose of art as a vehicle for uplifting the human spirit." Posters of the art in this book are available from awakeningarts.com.

Research, writing and illustrations for this book were generously supported by a grant from the Infinity Foundation.

Author's Acknowledgments

This story was first nurtured in the hills of northwestern New Jersey at Genesis Farm. Its founder, Miriam MacGillis, and Jean and Larry Edwards introduced me to the writings of Thomas Berry and Brian Swimme, and to a new way of integrating science and spirituality. Rajiv Malhotra, president of the Infinity Foundation, pointed me toward resources on eastern perspectives of evolution. Arthur Kosowsky, Ph.D., my neighbor and a Rutgers cosmologist, gave hours of advice as did Princeton University physicists Drs. Gillian Knapp, James Gunn, Michael Strauss, and Neil deGrass Tyson. Evolutionary biologist, Connie Barlow, taught me the language of Earth and children. Muffy Weaver and Glenn Hovemann, owners of Dawn Publications, leapt into the abyss in committing to co-create this unusual book. There have been many other co-creators of all ages. To name a few: Soren Rasmussen, Samuel and Toby Afron, Shelle Sumners, Ian Kalish, Hannah and Brad Wilson, Kate and Christine Alexander, Sara Van Wiegman, Mihovil Zuzul, Christopher and Katherine Scott, Sr. Maureen Wild, Lara Greenspan, Gina Cawley, Chris Reed, Naomi Brower, Ato Baffoe, Bruce Afron, Peter Knipe, Nancy Johnson, Ph.D., Sr. Gail Worcelo, Betty Fleming, Margery Cuyler, Maria Myers, Mary Coelho, Ralph Copleman, Susan Curry, Robert Wallis, Roger Martindell, Karen Giroux, Ph.D., Uta Krogman, Ph.D., Helene van Rasmussen, Joan Ogden, Ph.D., Theresa Maresca, Sue Steidel, Cynthia Cordes, Herb Simmens, Alissa Gerber, Amy Hansen, Judy Straub, Ph.D., Brenda Dunne, Ph.D., Karen Chaffee, Ph.D, Greg Nowak, Jeremy K. Taylor, Libby Kelley, Michelle Jacobs, and Allyson Owen. For marathon Morgan family brainstorms, I thank Maureen, John, Douglas, Frissie, Amalia, Seth, Lael, Brian, Eric, Rebecca, Adele, Mike, Willard and Sarah. To all the people I talked to on the streets of Princeton, whose names I don't even know, thank you for sharing precious moments. Thanks also to the Nevada City School of the Arts and the Ananda Living Wisdom School of Nevada City, California. And though he'll probably shrug his shoulders when he hears this, I am profoundly grateful to my son, Morgan Martindell, for moments in the dark, telling bedtime stories and for being my chief ten-year-old collaborator. We have traveled the Universe, my sweet Morgady, haven't we!

Dawn Publications offers children's books that encourage an appreciation for the web of life on Earth.

ALSO BY JENNIFER MORGAN, ILLUSTRATED BY DANA LYNNE ANDERSEN

From Lava to Life: The Universe Tells Our Earth Story—The second book in the Universe series tells of how Earth triumphs over crisis to become bacteria. . . jellyfish. . . flowers. . . dinosaurs. . . and the very first mammals.

Mammals Who Morph: The Universe Tells Our Evolution Story (Book Three) The last in the series picks up with the extinction of dinosaurs, and tells how tiny mammals survived and morphed into lots of new Earthlings . . . horses, whales and a kind of mammal with a powerful imagination—you.

The "Earth Heroes" Series is a collection of 24 intriguing biographies that will educate, fascinate, and inspire readers. Three books spotlight eight of the world's most renowned naturalists, with a particular emphasis on how the subjects' childhoods helped them to develop interests and passions that later guided them into their groundbreaking work, often in spite of great obstacles.

> *Earth Heroes: Champions of the Wilderness*
>
> *Earth Heroes: Champions of the Ocean*
>
> *Earth Heroes: Champions of Wild Animals*

Girls Who Looked Under Rocks. Six girls, from the 17th to the 20th century, didn't run from spiders or snakes but crouched down to take a closer look. They became pioneering naturalists, scientists, and writers.

Dandelion Seed's Big Dream. This "weed" seed flies with beauty, survives storms, endures darkness, never gives up. It is one of nature's greatest success stories that makes the world a brighter place.

The Prairie That Nature Built. A wild prairie is a lively place in this rhythmic romp with munchers and crunchers above and below the grasses so thick, and fires that flare, and rains that quench—and always the prairie grows green.

The "One Community" Series takes a close look at "communities" of animals and how they get along, in several fascinating habitats:

> *Under One Rock: Bugs, Slugs and Other Ughs*
>
> *In One Tidepool: Crabs, Snails and Salty Tails*
>
> *Near One Cattail: Turtles, Logs and Leaping Frogs*
>
> *On One Flower: Butterflies, Ticks and a few More Icks*

Dawn Publications is dedicated to inspiring in children a deeper understanding and appreciation for all life on Earth. To view our full list of titles, or to order, please visit our web site at www.dawnpub.com, or call 800-545-7475.